INTRODUCTION

Kumi and Chanti are two African children. They have been given great magical powers and sent on a very special mission. Their mission is to be the caretakers of African-American history. And, they are to take this history to the children of the world.

Kumi is eight, his sister, Chanti is six. They can travel all over the world through space and time. In so doing, they watch and record true stories. Stories about great African-American lives and deeds.

When Kumi and Chanti touch the golden chairs they wear, they can fly. When they sprinkle themselves with their special dust, they can become invisible. When they use their magic twigs, they can change into anything they wish.

Join Kumi and Chanti in their exciting world of African-American history!

This story is about George Washington Carver!

"GEORGE WASHINGTON CARVER"

Published by Empak Enterprises, Inc.
212 East Ohio Street, Chicago, IL 60611

Publisher & Editor: Richard L. Green
Writer: LaVerne C. Johnson
Assoc. Editor: Deborah A. Green
Production: Dickinson & Associates, Inc.
Illustration: Craig Rex Perry

Hurry Chanti, we have a wonderful story to tell!

I know Kumi, it is about the man who made many things out of peanuts and sweet potatoes.

George Washington Carver and his mother and brother were slaves on a small Missouri farm. George would one day grow up to be one of the greatest scientists in the world.

One night, the baby George and his mother were stolen by slave kidnappers called "Night Riders."

4

Look Chanti, little George has been brought home.

I wonder where George's mother is, Kumi?

Moses Carver, the farmer who owned George, was able to get George back. As a reward, Moses gave the men who returned little George a racehorse. George's mother was never seen again.

5

The father of George and his older brother, Jim, had died when they were very young. Now their mother, Mary, was gone from their lives. They wondered if they would be allowed to remain with the Carver family.

George and his brother look so sad.

They miss their mother, Chanti.

Mr. and Mrs. Carver do not have any children.

Well, they do now!

The Carvers raised George and his brother Jim, as their very own sons. The Carvers were very kind and loving people.

8

George was not as strong as his brother, Jim. Jim helped with the farming. The Carvers let George help in the house and in the garden.

He seems to know how to make everything grow, doesn't he Chanti?

Young George soon became known as the "Plant Doctor" because he knew so much about plants. Neighbors brought their sick plants to him for help.

George loved the woods near his house.
So, he started a garden in the woods.
Every chance he got, he would work
with plants in his little garden.

George needs a special teacher?

Yes, he has learned as much as he can on his own.

Because George was so very smart, the Carvers sent him to a private teacher. There were no schools for Black children in Diamond Grove, Missouri.

Kumi, the Carvers do not want to see George leave. They think that he is too young.

Chanti, he has to go. He wants to go to school!

Finally, George left the Carvers' home to go to a Black school in Neosho, Missouri. At the age of 12, he was on his own.

George has made a lot of friends in his new school.

They like him because he is such a good person.

A year later, George moved to Kansas. There, he went to several high schools. Even though the children at these schools were White, George made many friends.

Kumi, I think George works too hard.

George has never been afraid of hard work. He has to earn his keep, Chanti.

To earn a living, George did all kinds of work. He cooked. He did laundry. He did housework. And, he worked as a farmhand.

But, Kumi, the college told George that they would be glad to have him.

They did not know the color of his skin, Chanti.

George finished high school and went to Highland, Kansas to go to college. Highland College turned George away because it did not accept Black students.

Well, George finally got into college!

I know that he would keep trying until he made it, Chanti.

George was set on going to college! A few years later, he entered Simpson College in Iowa to study art. He was their first Black student.

The next year, Mr. Carver went to the college that is now Iowa State University. He worked there as a janitor to pay for his schooling.

Even though he was busy with school, Mr. Carver never gave up his artwork. He still found time to paint beautiful pictures of flowers and plants.

Kumi, do the White students care that their teacher is Black?

No Chanti, Mr. Carver is such a great teacher.

Mr. Carver was a top student at Iowa State. He received two degrees. He also became one of Iowa State's best teachers. However, he really wanted to help and teach Black students.

Dr. Carver accepted Booker T. Washington's teaching offer. He was finally able to teach Black students. He was a wonderful teacher. The students loved him.

Planting cotton in the very same places every year had ruined the soil in the South. Carver told the farmers that instead of cotton, they should sometimes plant other crops, such as peanuts, sweet potatoes, peas, and clover. This would make the soil healthy again.

Some of Dr. Carver's most famous work was done in his laboratory. He called his lab "God's Little Workshop." Every day he prayed before going inside. He said, "God was his guide!"

It's hard to believe that Dr. Carver made so many things from peanuts.

He also made many things from sweet potatoes and pecans, Chanti.

In his lab, Dr. Carver made over 300 products from the peanut. Things like instant coffee, milk, cream, peanut butter, cooking oil, paper, paint, flour, and much more.

Cream

COOKING
OIL

DYE

This is the Carver Museum at Tuskegee! I'm glad there are many places and things to remind us of him, Kumi.

Dr. Carver was a great scientist and African-American.

Dr. George Washington Carver died at Tuskegee on January 5, 1943. He never accepted money for his discoveries. He gave his knowledge to the people of the world. He showed them how to make useful products from everyday things.

Many schools have been named for Dr. Carver. A stamp was issued in his honor. And, the place where he was born a slave is now a national monument!

Spread the Word:
Catalog now available
on the Internet
www.empakpub.com